Faithbuilders

A Bouquet of Blessings

by Doreen Harrison

To Jakey,

As you bless others, may you be blessed too!
You are the sunshine in people's life!

Brother
Mark
- x -

P.S. we are all blossoming like flowers!

A Bouquet of Blessings by Doreen Harrison

First Published in Great Britain in 2015

FAITHBUILDERS PUBLISHING www.biblestudiesonline.org.uk

An Imprint of Apostolos Publishing Ltd,
3rd Floor, 207 Regent Street,
London W1B 3HH
www.apostolos-publishing.com

British Library Cataloguing-in-Publication Data

A catalogue record for this book is available from the British Library

ISBN: 978-1-910942-12-3

Cover Design by Blitz Media, Pontypool, Torfaen

Cover Image © Maximus Vonet| Dreamstime Stock Photos.

Other stock photo illustrations used under license and are credited throughout.

Printed and bound in Great Britain by Marston Book Services Limited, Oxfordshire.

Dedicated to all those who (like me) are of senior years.

Contents

When I became 80 years old I noticed a subtle difference in attitude towards me—even amongst my family and close friends! I had not changed — but perception of how to treat someone of that age turned me — overnight — into a little old lady who needed extra care and consideration!

Arthritis, diabetes and macular degeneration do require extra attention, but I am active and enthusiastic as I approach each new day. For me, my age is surely a proof of words in Psalm 31. "I trust you, O Lord. I say, you are my God. My times are in your hands.

This is a collection of anecdotes, poems and stories. It is a privilege to have been alive for 80 years, and the title of the book is "80, Not Out!" I know that "I am in His hands - whate'er the future holds, I'm in His hands".

This is a book with particular purpose for elderly people, but since none of us can hold back the passing of the years, it may offer valuable wisdom for everyone! I hope you enjoy reading it as much as I have enjoyed putting it together!

The Hands of God

The waiting room table usually held a variety of up to date magazines, but today it was empty. Instead of the welcome reading material was a single notice. Because of the possibility of contracting swine flu, the doctor's surgery had been advised to remove all magazines as a health and safety precaution. Well, I was in this particular waiting room for reasons of my health and so I should perhaps be pleased about the attempts to keep me healthy!

But I think today's society has become overwhelmingly concerned with health and safety. I recently read an article about a school crossing patrol man who had wielded his lollipop for several years, but who was facing suspension for giving "high fives" to the children who had become his friends. How sad, I thought, that friendliness at work has become so unacceptable.

Some time ago my husband and I visited a cathedral where each pew contained a notice concerning 'sharing the peace'. Worshippers were advised not to shake hands in case they shared germs in the process. It appears that even hand to hand contact has become dangerous! In some situations it is no longer considered advisable for adults to say to a child, "hold my hand" in case such might be misinterpreted as being sinister. The helping hands of our health care professionals reach out to us in protective gloves.

Many years ago, I recollect a lecturer at teacher training college reminding us to wash our hands in soap and water frequently, for "you never know where the children's hands have been before they reached yours!" Yet at the same time we were encouraged to express our concern and interest with the friendly touch of a human hand.

I have always treasured the words written by Minnie Haskins, quoted by King George VI in his broadcast to the Commonwealth in 1939:

> *"Go out into the darkness and put your hand into the hand of God. That shall be better to you than light and safer than a known way."*

If today's society presents us with a multitude of doubts and fears, it is good to remember that God never changes and we are safe with him. Rabbi Ben Ezra once wrote: *"Our times are in his hand. Trust God, nor be afraid."*

Consider this verse from Psalm 37: *"The Lord makes firm the steps of the one who delights in him; though he may stumble, he will not fall, for the Lord upholds him with his hand."*

Our Ripening Years

Nowadays, old age seems to be postponed until people are well into their nineties. We should all be delighted by this! It seems that the welfare state, state pension pot, the functions of the National Health Service, all contribute to our continuing health and quality of life.

But what about those people who deteriorate in mind and body and become depressed in spirit? Depression in the elderly is a truly bleak situation. C. S. Lewis wrote of his old age, "I am no longer complete!" For some old people this is an apt description of their feelings. When partners and friends have passed away, and other family members are far apart—perhaps even in another country—old people can feel isolated and alone.

Once upon a time, people gathered for companionship in local chapels and churches – but with more and more places of worship closing, we are denied even that lifeline. Maybe we feel that even the ability to pray and worship God is something lost to us. But the good news is that God is always ready to listen to people, and he has plenty of people willing to lend a listening ear to the elderly if we give them an opportunity to do so.

What will they hear from us?

They will hear our memories. This is one of the reasons why sheltered accommodation can be such a good option, with groups of people who share common memories. Counsellors sometimes speak of "growing fat on the past" and a life without memories to share would be very lean and empty. To those who are dismissive, who think "Oh no! We've heard it all before!" I would say, please indulge the elderly, allow us to reminisce, and savour our memories—you may learn much from them.

They will also hear all about our problems! Our increasing age makes it difficult to walk—arthritic limbs stop us taking part in activities we have enjoyed for many years. Our sight fails and so does our hearing; our minds slow down so that we are less accurate in our response to questions. That's why people think we're past it! But we're not 'past it' at all!

The message of creation is that each year ends in a blaze of autumn glory. All an apple has to do, after all the hard work of growing, swelling and ripening — is to allow people to admire and enjoy its ripeness and wealth of beauty! Such should the experience of our old age.

The Next Generation

Have you ever experienced getting to the top of the stairs, only to realise you had forgotten what you went up for?

Well, recently on the TV news I heard of a musician who forgot his $300,000 violin, which he had left in a taxi on his way home from a concert. Only after supper and a shower did he recollect that when he left the concert hall he was carrying the valuable instrument! It was much later in the evening that he managed to retrieve it. That certainly puts my forgetful times into perspective!

Reaching the top of the stairs or reaching the end of the day could be used as metaphors for growing old. There is of course one great question in life: 'What is it all about?' Our lives so often seem to be out of tune, and we do not know how to make the music of harmonious living. I wonder if the reason for this might be that we have forgotten something valuable in this 21st century: we have forgotten the value of God's promises.

The Bible gives us all a reason for living – even when we reach our senior years! Psalm 71 says:

> *As for me I will always have hope; I will praise you more and more. Even when I am old and grey, do not forsake me, my God till I declare your power to the next generation, your mighty acts to all who are to come*

Almost every day we hear news reports which contain dire predictions concerning numbers of people being affected by Alzheimer's disease and about the rising cost of our residential care; but the Bible gives us a much more positive outlook. There is a reason for living - we are to be an example to the next generation. Their enterprise and enthusiasm for worship and service should be the result of our continuing testimony to the unfailing love of God.

Psalm 78 says:

> *I will utter hidden things, things from of old—things we have heard and known, things our ancestors have told us. We will not hide them from their descendants;* **we will tell the next generation** *the praiseworthy deeds of the Lord, his power, and the wonders he has done.*

Everlasting Security

My granddaughter enjoyed her work experience at a residential home. Having been asked to massage the residents hands, she approached one elderly lady, "May I gently stroke your hand?" The lady replied, eagerly, "Oh yes, you can! Actually, I have two of them - I don't know where they came from, but I've got them right here!"

We smile when old people produce such unique statements. We care deeply when someone we love begins to forget things and make simple mistakes. The touch of a hand can bring such comfort — but there is even more comfort to be found in the pages of the Bible. These sacred pages contain immeasurable resources of infinite comfort. Here are just a few:

> ""Wisdom is with aged men, with long life is understanding. With Him are wisdom and might; To

Him belong counsel and understanding." (Job 12:12-13)

"Neither height nor depth, nor anything else in all creation, will be able to separate us from the love of God that is in Christ Jesus our Lord.."(Rom. 8:39)

"God has said, 'Never will I leave you; never will I forsake you.'" (Heb. 13:5)

I recently read an account, written by a Christian minister working with elderly patients who seemed completely passive and incapable of thinking. He would gently speak to them, telling them that Jesus loved them. It did not bother him that all their senses seemed to have gone. This is how he explains his ministry. "Each person is precious to God. For a short time the inner being is behind an invisible veil of unawareness. The body might be deteriorating, but not so the eternal life within. That will live forever."

Just as the lady my granddaughter was helping, had forgotten her hands, so it can be easy sometimes to forget the God who reaches out his hands to help us. His words of comfort tell of mighty hands which are available to each of us, they are underneath and all around us.

The eternal God is your refuge, and underneath are the everlasting arms. (Deut. 33:27)

We may not be able to understand the greatness of God's care, but as the lady said of her own hands, the same is true of God's hands underneath and all around you - "I don't know where they came from — but I've got them, right here!"

© Galina Barskaya | Dreamstime.com

Spring in My Soul

An insurance salesman called on an elderly couple and tried to persuade them that they needed security for the next 10 years of their lives. The old man replied, "Son, at our age we don't even buy green bananas!"

The only absolute certainty for any of us is that one day our life will come to an end. However, unlike other milestones in life's journey, we do not find it easy to prepare for the final one.

Books are written on bringing up children, marriage guidance, middle age crisis, the trauma of chronic illness, managing on a pension, but I have yet to find any books which deal with the subject of growing old gracefully – except, of course, for the Bible.

Psalm 71 says:

> *O God, You have taught me from my youth, And I still declare Your wondrous deeds. And even when I am old and grey, O God, do not forsake me, Until I declare Your strength to this generation, Your power to all who are to come. (Psalm 71:17-18)*

Whenever I hear, or read, a discussion concerning today's young people and the way in which society is going, I am reminded of these words. Those of us who are elderly were taught to respect God and honour his word, and it is one of our responsibilities to pass on what we have learned to the next generation.

When I was a teenager, I used to visit an elderly lady in our village called Mrs Honey. She was bed ridden and often in pain but invariably her demeanour was as sweet as her name.

One hot summer's day I called in and I was describing to her my plans for a holiday. She listened patiently and then she spoke. She said, "I am looking forward to a most wonderful holiday." I looked at her — in disbelief really. She smiled and then explained, "My dear, one day soon I will be on my way to heaven!"

Possibly some in our modern generation might think Mrs. Honey was "bananas!" But we must never allow our faith to become old and grey when God intends us to have a fresh joy in his presence every day, so that in spite of age it is always springtime in our soul!

© Anna Omelchenko| Dreamstime.com

A Child in Old Age

When Elizabeth married Zechariah, it was a sunny day and everyone was happy for the pretty bride and her handsome bridegroom. Elizabeth walked to her new home under a canopy of flowers. Friends held the four corners of the canopy and it was full of roses, lilies, stephanotis, sweet smelling blossoms and leaves. People gave her presents and one of the special gifts was a white shawl, carefully folded with sprigs of lavender. "For your first baby," read the note which was tucked into the shawl.

Elizabeth looked forward to being a mother. "Maybe I will have a baby son," she thought, "with black curly hair, like Zechariah has - or perhaps a baby daughter and I will name her Elizabeth Ruth!" She often unwrapped the shawl and imagined how she would feel, cuddling the soft folds around her very own baby.

The years went by, and no baby was born. Elizabeth grew older, her hair turned grey, and one day she shook out the shawl and wrapped it around her own shoulders. She said, "I am too old now to have a baby and the shawl is too pretty to waste." But although it was comfortable to feel the soft white shawl against her skin when cold winds blew, Elizabeth always remembered that this shawl was really meant for a baby's comfort, and sometimes she wiped away a tear with a corner of the shawl as she thought of the baby that had never been born to her and Zechariah.

Zechariah was a priest. Twice a year he was called to the Temple in Jerusalem to share in the worship there. Elizabeth always made sure that he his official robes were well pressed and that his hair was neatly trimmed. It was a great honour to be part of the Temple ceremonies and she wanted Zechariah to look his best. If Zechariah was chosen to burn incense in the part of the Temple called the Holy of Holies, Elizabeth knew that he would come home smelling of the fragrance of incense and that even his beard would carry the fragrance.

Before the ceremonies began, the priests were appointed to their duties and Zechariah was proud to be invited to take the incense into the Holy of Holies and burn it there. It was an important duty, and Zechariah had never been chosen before.

The crowd of worshippers who were at the temple that day waited outside because only the priest was allowed to go through the special entrance to burn incense. Zechariah went through the door. It was quiet inside -- quite dim, because there were no windows. Zechariah took the incense in his hand and approached the altar.

Suddenly, the place was filled with brilliant white light, and there stood an angel. Zechariah couldn't move—this was incredible. The angel reached out a hand towards him. "Do not be afraid, Zechariah, your prayers have been answered," he said. Zechariah looked at the glorious, shining, glowing angel. "What prayer does he mean?" he thought.

The angel smiled. "Your wife Elizabeth is going to have a baby", he said.

"He will be a special son; God is giving him the responsibility of preparing the way for Messiah. You are chosen to be the parents of John."

Zechariah looked again at the angel. He thought of all the years that he and Elizabeth had longed to have a baby of their own. He thought about Elizabeth's grey hair and how she used a stick to walk across to the village well, on account of her arthritis.

"How can I be sure of this? We are both old now," he told the angel.

Never argue with an angel! The shining figure seemed to glow even more brightly "I am Gabriel," he answered. "I have come from the presence of God with this message for you and now, so that you will not be able to share your doubts with anyone else— you will be dumb until your son is born."

When Zechariah came out of the Holy of Holies, blinking in the sunlight and unable to speak, the waiting people realised that something unusual had happened and they were very quick to worship God that day because they were not sure what would happen next.

Elizabeth read about the angel as Zechariah wrote the whole account out for her as soon as he got home. At first she didn't believe the angels message, but as the weeks went by she realised that she was going to have a baby -- and one day she took the shawl, the wedding present shawl, and carefully washed it and then folded it, with sprigs of lavender, so that it would be sweet for her baby.

When he was born, and swaddled so delightfully in the shawl, she held him up for everyone to see, and Zechariah's voice came back as he proudly wrote these words: "His name is John."

John the Baptist was Gods messenger to prepare the way for Jesus. He was a special child. But then each of us is special to God, and even when we grow old, we must realise that like John, we are put on this planet for a purpose!

© Lowsun | Dreamstime.com

A Prayer for Peace

My Granddad was a Sergeant Major in the First World War, and he had medals to prove it! He never spoke about those terrible experiences, the mud and the trenches, and he only ever shared one army experience with his family.

When he was demobbed, he took on the management of a small community establishment in a Northern Industrial town. One morning, in the local market, someone called out to him. "Sergeant Major, stand at ease!" Turning, he saw his ex-Commanding Officer, in full dress uniform. "Sergeant Major, this is to say thank you for loyal service!" and he handed Granddad a small parcel, saluted him and disappeared into the crowd. The parcel contained a pair of binoculars—which my Granddad would display and use with pride and pleasure.

Granddad's establishment was a place where you could take your family, where you were always sure of a welcome and where you would feel safe. The war was over and he was working for peace in peace time. His greatest asset was my Grandma. She was a small, rosy-faced lady, with grey curly hair and she believed in prayer. Granddad had good intentions and Grandma intended that good should come of those intentions! She followed the advice of the Bible:

> "I urge, then, first of all, that petitions, prayers, intercession and thanksgiving be made for all people—for kings and all those in authority, that we may live peaceful and quiet lives in all godliness and holiness."

I realise that binoculars can be used to magnify or they can be used to diminish. As I write, the events of World War I are being magnified. As we remember the heroic events of two World Wars, we can identify heavenly interventions such as Dunkirk, when our little boats evacuated an army under the very noses— and gun barrels—of our German enemies. Yet as we rightly remember deeds of valour, we must not fail to remember that there were times of despair, devastation and horrible death. It is still true that war solves nothing. Even after the horrors of two World Wars, fighting continues to this hour around the world.

I recall my Grandma as an ordinary lady, who prayed for her family and friends; bringing peace into the small corner of her world. I think that the challenge for the present time is that we should pray for peace where we live, and in the world. Prayer has a magnificent record of amazing success!

Grandad's War

My Granddad fought in the First World War
But he never spoke of the blood and the gore,
The mud in the trenches, of death and despair—
Sufficient to tell us, "Oh, yes, I was there!"

He could polish his medals, display them with pride,
But stories of warfare were kept stored inside.
"Fair fighting is face to face," he would say,
"Not button press, thousands dead, like war today!"

He had twirly whiskers. He walked with a spring
In his step. He loved music. We liked him to sing
"Roll out the barrel!" A strong melody! He
Tenored dramatically. His mug of tea

Held a large splash of whiskey. He liked a cigar
At times he got merry. My Mum then said, "Pa,
Remember, the kids are here, listening to you!"
We'd attend well to Granddad, and learn what he knew.

Ask, "What was it like, going over the hill?"
At this our dear Granddad became very still;
With a pause before saying, "Just go out to play!"
"I don't feel like answering questions! Away!"

I have memories of World War Two, fear World War
Three,
Apprehensive and anxious. This horror will be
Mushroom cloud mayhem, a devilish dance;
No longer a war that allows any chance
To the side who is hit first. I understand now.

Why my Granddad fell silent and furrowed his brow;
And didn't embellish his wartime career —
Such sickening sagas brings nobody cheer.
A gentle old soldier, his duty well done,
He did not give war glamour; nor should anyone!

© Atee83 | Dreamstime.com

The Snowdrop

At the entrance to our house where we keep the various refuse bins, is a patch of ground on which snowdrops flower each spring. Every year, they manage to survive the banging of the bins, the frequent attention of passing dogs, the battering of wind and rain, the heat of summer sunshine (when we have any!) and they are delightful reminders that "winter is past- sweet spring has come, at last!"

We didn't plant them, they just appeared there, years ago, and we have allowed them to flourish where they are, a beautiful reminder each year that "Spring always follows winter."

Their botanical name, Galanthus, comes from the Greek words, gala (milk) and anthus (flower). Someone who collects, grows or delights in snowdrops is called a Galanthophile. On Valentine's day 2014, a lady paid £1,602 to name a new species of snowdrop as a tribute to her grandfather.

Recently we were invited to a 99th birthday party, and it was a wonderful occasion! There were five generations of family there, friends, a male voice choir from Cardiff to serenade the dear old man whose birthday we were celebrating, delicious food, birthday balloons and party poppers. He even had a cake shaped like the number 99! And there, on each table, growing in little pots, were snowdrops, transplanted for the day from a relative's garden!

The snowdrops at the birthday party were a lovely tribute to a gentleman in the winter time of life whose personality still embodies the hope and happiness of spring!

There is a Proverb which states, "Anxiety weighs down the heart, but a kind word cheers it up" (Prov. 12:25). Snowdrops are like a collection of kind words. Do you recollect the song which suggested, "It costs so little, but it means so much —when you greet a friend with a smile. A few kind words go a long, long way to make this life worthwhile!" Consider how different any society would be if we began to greet even our enemies with kind words!

When God presented Jesus to the world, His kind Words became flesh. The presence of Jesus can be with us through every winter of discontent, leading us to the joy of spring!

Midnight Music

The Bible tells of two Christian missionaries, Paul and Silas, who were falsely accused of causing a riot and for that reason they were thrown into prison. In those days sentences were harsh. They were severely flogged and then shackled in the inner cell of the prison. This was where condemned prisoners were put; doubtless the next dawn would be the last one they would ever see. How did they cope? The record of their predicament reads like this:

> *"About midnight Paul and Silas were praying and singing hymns to God, and the other prisoners were listening to them." (Acts 16:25)*

Well, they certainly had a captive audience, but to sing at such a dark hour requires personal response of a specific kind. Unable to settle to sleep, due to the lacerations on their back caused by the whipping, they kept their spirits up by singing hymns. The fact that the other prisoners were listening and not shouting them down indicates that their singing was well worth hearing! Instead of abject fear they were expressing complete composure and even peace!

Suddenly there was a violent earthquake. The foundations of the prison were shaken and the prison doors flew open. Everybody's chains came loose. This did not happen because of the volume of the singing nor as a result of its quality! Two fine high voices might shatter a glass but are not likely to make the earth shake. Consider, then, the subject of their song. They were singing hymns to God!

The power of God is such that He is recorded as speaking into darkness and saying "Let there be light!" and then there was light! In their midnight experience, Paul and Silas were able to sing because they trusted God. When the darkness of their situation and circumstances obscured the light of hope, they remembered that nothing can extinguish faith.

The Bible asks a question: "What can separate us from the love of God in Christ Jesus our Lord?" (Romans 8:35) and it gives the answer:

> "For I am convinced that neither death nor life, neither angels nor demons, neither the present nor the future, nor any powers, neither height nor depth, nor anything else in all creation, will be able to separate us from the love of God that is in Christ Jesus our Lord." (Rom. 8:38-39)

That is why Paul and Silas were able to sing at midnight!

The Power of a Word

There is a well-known story in the Bible concerning the tribe of Ephraim, who were captured one by one by the other Israelites during a civil war simply because they lisped!

The Israeli sentry would stop people at the ford over the Jordan and command them to say the word "Shibboleth." If the man was from Ephraim he would answer, "Sibboleth" because people from Ephraim could not pronounce the word correctly. The Bible says that 42,000 Ephraimites were captured in this way! Such can be the power of a word.

(You may read the whole story in Judges chapter 12).

In Canterbury cathedral there is a monument to Thomas a Becket, on the place where he was murdered. The King, exasperated by something that the Archbishop had done, remarked, "Who will rid me of this turbulent priest?" and a listening soldier decided to do what the king had requested His Majesty's idle words produced a horrific sequel.

I once had a very old film projector which came with several free clips of film. One of these films showed a crowded room and a commanding old lady who remarked tersely, "Go!" and all at once all the people left the room! I used to play this clip to myself over and over again, being fascinated by the power of a single word.

The Bible has a magnificent beginning. It records the powerful words of God the creator. In Genesis chapter 1 we read, "And God said, Let there be light; and there was light!" Surely there can be no greater power than is resident in the Word of the Living God.

Today, as I write, the sky is blue and the sun is bright; a definite proof of the power of those words, and an affirmation that "the word of the Lord endures for ever."

In an age of change and challenge, there is one absolute certainty, and that is, there will be night after day and morning after the night. God promised Noah that as long as the earth remains there will be day and night. His love and mercy are given us afresh every morning.

Body, Mind and Spirit

In the present climate of Health and Safety precautions, a young boy was anxious about the rights and wrongs of floating Moses in a basket on the river Nile. 'What about the crocodiles?" he asked "Suppose they eat him?" Another boy gave a quick reply, "Well, of course they wouldn't!" he said. "God would make sure they were vegetarian crocodiles!"

This week I read that our healthy target of eating five fruit and veg a day has been increased to seven. Seven is the perfect number, but doubtless time will increase the target as the obesity statistics rise and Health and safety zooms into action over our food consumption.

Cabbage, cauliflower, carrots and celery will never replace cream cheese, chocolate, coronation chicken and cupcakes, but certainly there is wisdom in making sure we have a balanced diet and take care of our body; after all, it is the carrier of our immortal soul. We are body, soul and mind and all three aspects of our humanity require care and attention if we are to live healthy and safe lives.

I was with a friend the other day who is 94 years old. She told me, "I have worked hard all my life and kept my body active -- maybe that is why I've lasted so long" She was a school governor until she was 90 years old and takes a lively interest in local affairs. She enjoys company and holds a good conversation with everyone she meets. And for much of her life she has been an active member of a small church here in the South Wales valleys; her body, mind and spirit are in good balance and she is a delight to know.

Three verses from Psalm 13 hold the three aspects in balance:

"I trust in your unfailing love." When we trust in God we are using our mind. "My heart rejoices in your salvation." The heart represents our body. "I will sing the Lord's praise, for he has been good to me" is a spiritual response to a God who is concerned for our wellbeing.

I once heard a modern translation of the verse which goes something like this "I'm singing at the top of my lungs, I'm so full of answered prayers!" Of course, if we want proof that God answers prayer, then we must to pray.

Let's start right away!

© Tupungato | Dreamstime.com

A Story of Ancient Egypt

Long ago, in the land of Egypt, the people of Israel were slaves to the Egyptians. However, they were strong and healthy, and there were many of them. Pharaoh, the leader of the Egyptians, feared the Israelites and made a wicked plan.

"There are too many Israelites around!" he declared. "In future, every Hebrew baby boy shall be thrown into the river Nile as soon as he is born."

Underneath the steps which led from Pharaoh's palace to the edge of the Nile, there lurked an old crocodile whose name was Cruncher. He wallowed in the mud, and only his snout and his wicked eyes showed above the water. Cruncher seldom moved. He lay in the mud and he lived on kitchen scraps which the palace servants threw into the water every morning. He ate breakfast bits, luncheon leftovers, and supper scraps. He ate pieces of partridge, pigeon, peacock pie, pineapples, pomegranates, peaches and purple popcorn. He ate bits of bones, slimy skin and fatty fragments. He sank deeper and deeper into the mud under the palace steps, and through all the long afternoons he dreamed of the day when he would be able to sink his old yellow teeth into the soft sweet flesh - of a human baby. He was not a nice crocodile!

Near to the palace, there lived an Israelite family. There was a son, daughter and a baby boy, who was yet to be named. The family hid their baby from Pharaoh's men for three months. By then he was too noisy to keep hidden any longer, and every day his life was in danger. Being desperate, the mother prayed to God about the situation, and as she did so, the thought came to her that she should put the baby into the water herself, and trust God to take care of him. So she made a little basket and coated it with pitch, to make it waterproof. Then she put her baby boy into the basket, and placed it carefully into the reeds at the edge of the river. Her daughter Miriam stayed on the river bank to watch over the baby, whilst the mother went home to pray.

Down in the mud, Cruncher saw the basket. His nose twitched and his eyes opened wide! He could smell a baby! "Oh bliss, oh rapture," he said to himself, "packed lunch today! A baby in a basket!" He lunged forward, to crunch and munch the baby, but he couldn't move. He was stuck fast in the mud like an old wrecked ship. He heaved and pulled, but the mud held him firmly.

At that precise moment, the Princess of Egypt came gracefully along the river bank with some of her maids in waiting. She saw the basket, and sent one of her servants to fetch it. Cruncher was furious as he watched his packed lunch being lifted out of the water. He sank back into the mud and real crocodile tears slid down his snout, splashing into the river. The baby was crying too; he was cold, hungry and missing his mother. The princess lifted him out of the basket, and he looked up at her in surprise. She had a pretty face and she was smiling sweetly at him. One of the long feathers in her headdress brushed against his cheek and he reached up a chubby fist to touch it. The princess cuddled him close. "This baby needs looking after," she said, "so I shall make sure he is safe."

Miriam heard all this, and ran down the steep steps to the princess. "Excuse me," she said, "I saw you with the baby, and I wondered if you needed a child minder to help you to look after him? I know a good one and she is free at the moment."

"What a helpful suggestion," said the princess. "I am always busy with palace duties and I will need someone to help me."

Miriam ran all the way home and told her mother what had happened. Her mother put on a clean apron and went with her to meet the princess. "I need a careful person to look after this baby for me," said the princess. But the baby had recognised his own mother's voice and he reached out his arms to her and chuckled with pleasure.

"His name is Moses," said the princess. "It means, 'Rescued from the water.'"

© Anke Van Wyk| Dreamstime.com

Will Someone Listen to Me?

Years ago, when I taught a class of infants, the formal accolade for good work was to go to the head teacher and receive a gold star. David never succeeded at anything, but one morning he produced work which was, for him, quite outstanding. "Take it to the headmaster," I said, "and tell him I'm pleased with you." I heard his heartrending sobs as he came back and handed me his book. No star, but a comment in the head teacher's writing, "Not good enough!" "Didn't you say that I was pleased with you?" I inquired. David answered sadly, "He didn't listen!"

How often we jump to conclusions? We judge by appearances and give no opportunity for others to tell their side of the story. Listening is a simple skill; we have been involved in listening since we were born. Listening must be one of the easiest things in the world, yet it is one of the hardest skills to practice properly.

I think we often listen with ears tuned to our own agenda, our own decisions, our previous history and our family background. Through the noise of these inner messages we are expected to interpret the words of another person, who carries a similar background colouring of experience, emotion and environment. Quite a complicated work of translation, wouldn't you agree? We listen with our eyes, too. Body language can speak louder than words. In the case of David, he bounced into the head teacher's room, face wreathed in smiles, book held out with glee. But the head teacher remembered previous encounters with David, and misinterpreted the body language. "This boy is brazen about his work," was the message the head teacher imagined. The spoken words were not heard because the boy's body language was misinterpreted.

We listen with our love. Who was to blame in the David saga? I was! I should have thought about David's previous sorties to the head's room, and preceded him with a brief note of explanation. "Today, David has done some presentable work and I am sending him along to show it to you." Love, concern, empathy, would have encouraged me to think carefully about the child I was dealing with. I would have thought about the stress of running a school, and not surmised that the head teacher could read my thoughts concerning David's work! I was responsible for the message which was misinterpreted. But I was not responsible for the one who misheard it. We have our own ears! So how do we listen? How do we correctly interpret what is being said to us? In our family setting, do we really understand what our spouse is saying? Let's be careful today to listen *properly*.

Treats for your Sweet-tooth!

I must confess to loving tea-time treats like this! But when I was growing up in an industrial town in Northern England, there were only two special tea time treats (if I'd been good)! One was a sandwich filled with sugar, the other a sandwich filled with chocolate; sweet rewards for good behaviour! In view of the fact that sugar is now said to be bad for you, perhaps my living beyond 80 is an indication of my lack of good behaviour? Apparently GPs believe that sugar is to be avoided when possible. It lurks in many foods; we are advised to read with care the label on each tin, jar, packet, bottle or box to ensure we are not taking too much. I wonder when the Valentine writers will be forced to rephrase the well-known verse: "Roses are red, violets are blue—sugar is sweet and I love you."

In view of present health information chocolate might no longer be considered an indication of undying love!

We all want to live healthy lives but I can't help wondering if all this preoccupation with health is a bit too much? Are we creating a 'sour' society? Surely there are occasions-- on most days-- when a sweetener of some kind would be most acceptable? Tea just isn't the same without it! In Psalm 119 we read:

"How sweet are your words to my taste, sweeter than honey to my mouth!" (Psalm 119:103)

And in Psalm 19, we read that God's words are:

"The fear of the Lord is pure, enduring forever. The decrees of the Lord are firm, and all of them are righteous. They are more precious than gold, than much pure gold; they are sweeter than honey, than honey from the honeycomb." (Psalm 19:9-10)

The sweet truth of God's grace and goodness to humankind should never be made to look sour by current opinion. The unfailing sweetness of God's grace is a certain antidote to all the cares and calamities of life.

When I reconsider the occasional excess of sugar in my childhood diet, it was because sugar was in short supply in those post war years of austerity. The fighting had finished, but the war was not over. Even so, in the battle of everyday living there need be no shortage of the sweet supply of the grace and goodness of God. Don't let public opinion diminish your appreciation of the sweetness of faith, hope and love. The words of the Lord are sweeter than honey, so try them for yourself!

Staying on Guard

My grandson was five when he came round to stay,
There's a box full of toys in our hall. He could play
With cars, bricks and aeroplanes, also he saw
A helmet, a breast plate, a sword, which he wore.

"I'm a Roman, look, Grandma!" He marched up and down,
Then turned to the garden, and said, with a frown,
"There's a cat, by that birds nest — I'm going to see."
And he charged, with his sword, and made that cat flee!

At five his concern was for birds that were small.
I trust that at fifteen, he'll still care for all
Who are threatened and frightened. Teenagers today
Have to cope with a world that is full of affray.

At school, with his peer group, where ever he goes
I hope early compassion will challenge for those
Who can't fight for themselves, who find growing up hard.
I trust that his creed is still, "Look! I'm on guard."

Thoughts from a Welsh Garden

It's a beautiful June day; the sky is blue and the sun shines on a bed of pink, red and yellow roses in our garden. I can see a pair of blackbirds busily foraging for food; I happen to know that they have a nest full of baby birds well hidden in our dense Wisteria tree! At the other side of the garden, long tailed tits are busy feeding their babies, whilst next door's cat reconnoitres the garden. Fortunately, the parent birds have chosen wise building sites and the little birds are safe from the predator. I can hear the birds, the rustle of the cat padding through the undergrowth, and the roar of traffic on the busy main road near our house! As I sit I appreciate all the sounds I hear. The traffic noise includes coaches taking pupils home from school, many cars and just a moment ago, a siren-blasting ambulance.

The coaches carry local children, I think to myself, who are being well educated with the possibility of professional careers for them all. Petrol is readily available for our cars, with maybe a 10 minute queue; compare that to the 10 hour wait described on the news yesterday for those in an oil rich country on another continent. The National Health Service continues to actively care for young and old in our nation without discrimination, whilst many from other countries struggle to pay a doctor. There are no tanks, no gun fire, no need to leave my home in panic to escape the results of anarchy and civil war.

Many people in other lands have fled their homes, leaving the comforts of civilisation behind to take up residence in makeshift refugee camps; without knowing how long such a situation will last. Here in our green and pleasant land, we are truly grateful for the privilege of our secure situation; we thank God daily for peace and relative political stability in our nation.

But what if all were to be taken from us, even as it has been taken from those in other lands? We have something which can never be taken away by war, famine or homelessness; the Christian's hope is something that will last forever.

> "Though the fig tree does not bud and there are no grapes on the vines, though the olive crop fails and the fields produce no food, though there are no sheep in the pen and no cattle in the stalls, yet I will rejoice in the Lord, I will be joyful in God my Savior." (Hab. 3:17-18)

As I sit in my Welsh garden, I am grateful more than ever for the presence of God which he reveals through nature and the world!

Lying Down in Green Pastures

It was a hot June morning, during a prolonged drought, when a small boy waved his reading book at me and said, "Miss, this book tells lies. It says, grass is green, but it isn't!" He pointed to the school field which was withered and yellow in the heat!

Green is a refreshing colour that sometimes gets a bad press; we say people are "green with envy," or we tell someone "don't be so green", implying that they are rather simple. Yet green is an energetic colour, it is the sign of living action and movement in nature and just like the traffic light of the same colour, its appearance in Spring tells us to get moving. Green is the colour of growth; after the Spring rains how green our valleys look! On the other hand, some people I know think green is an unlucky colour, and for that reason they will not wear it.

Green is a restful colour too; my eyesight is blessed to see a green landscape. The Bible uses the colour green to describe peace and contentment. Psalm 23 begins:

> *"The Lord is my shepherd, I lack nothing. He makes me lie down in green pastures."*

This Spring we have had a lot of rain which is why we are now surrounded by such an abundance of green growth. Psalm 23 picks up this thought, as it continues:

> *"He leads me beside quiet waters, he refreshes my soul."*

We live in a colourful world. God did not create a black and white landscape; he created it to be colourful for our pleasure. In the days of Noah, after the great Flood, in order to reassure the family as they came out of the Ark, God arched a rainbow over them and said:

> "I have set my rainbow in the clouds, and it will be the sign of the covenant between me and the earth."

As I enjoy the abundance of greenery in our valley; shades of lime green, emerald, turquoise, mint, sea green, dark, light and spring fresh and all of them so lovely, I am sure that the Bible is certainly a book which doesn't tell lies. It contains the truth about the God who loves us with an everlasting love; and who displays that love around us so that we may know him.

You are Never Surplus to Requirements

Years ago, as one of my holiday jobs, to supplement my college grant, I worked as an Orderly in a Geriatric hospital. We had 3 patients who had been evacuated from London during the war and no one ever reclaimed them. There was Mrs Antonelli, a tiny, lively Italian lady who had sold ice cream from a barrow. She was bed-ridden now. She loved to sing and she had an amazing repertoire of music-hall songs. Miss Targett was also bedridden. She was a gentle lady who never forgot to say thank you for even small kindnesses. Mrs Grey had osteoporosis. Her back was severely deformed and she was also bedridden. She was an accomplished seamstress and earned some money by sewing for the staff. As far as society was concerned it seemed as if these three ladies were surplus to requirements. However, what I learned from them was just as important as any of the lessons at college!

Mrs Antonelli had very little to sing about - but that did not stop her from singing. Miss Targett had very little reason to feel grateful for anything - but that didn't stop her saying thank you. Mrs Grey was terribly deformed: but her handiwork was incredibly beautiful. These were not three abandoned old people, they were three ladies who deserved respect and admiration for the way they accepted circumstances which they could not change. There is a surprising verse in the Bible which reads:

> "I have learned to be content whatever the circumstances" (Phil. 4:11)

I've you've been feeling a little sorry for yourself lately here is a fistful of blessings for you to consider:

First, you are still able to read this little book and understand what you are reading. Then secondly you we are alive; and thirdly, you have been allocated this day in which to enjoy being alive!

As a fourth blessing, we still live in a society where Churches are open for the worship and praise of the Lord God Almighty.

I hope you see that no one is ever surplus to God's requirements. He loved the world so much that He gave Jesus, His son, "so that whosoever believes in him will not perish but shall have eternal life." As we get older, it may well be that our circumstances will change, but God's love is a circumstance which will never change! That certainly is something to really sing about!

Contentment

What if our summer days, like wine,
Matured through hours of bright sunshine;
And olive groves climbed up to where,
We now rejoice in mountain air—
And rain was gauged in tiny spots,
Instead of somewhat larger pots!

What   if, on pavements clean and white
With cafes still alive at night,
By tables parasoled we sat
And talked and drank; and wondered at
Those distant lands in headlines shown
To have less lustre than our own.

What if we peered in looking glass,
And saw again that fresh young lass—
And lively lad, handsome and strong?
What if such wisdom as ours, the throng
Of fighting, feuding countries we
By agile politics made free?

What if we spoke with words of fire?
And if our singing, over choir,
Could rouse Eisteddfod epic sound?
And what if, slim instead of round
A marathon was but a stroll?
What if to gain, we lost our soul?

Our poetry ought not to bemoan
Such giftings as we cannot own;
But celebrate the destiny
Bequeathed to us communally.

These mountains sometimes veiled in grey,
Majestic at all times of day.
As wrinkles denote vibrant living,
Age and experience grandeur giving
What if our acre seems quite small?
Colour contentment over all;
Interweave with golden dreams,
Making a garment without seams.

Getting Inside the Banana!

An acquaintance of mine shared a most moving anecdote from their recent visit to a developing country. She watched a young girl, accompanied by a toddler, eat a banana—or at least, part of one!

The girl took the banana skin from a pile of rubbish and then, with infinite care, she peeled the skin until she had a handful of white pith which the toddler ate with real pleasure. Since I heard that story, I have viewed the very familiar fruit in a different way. To these two children in an area of great poverty, the discarded peel contained food—and gave me considerable food for thought!

Supermarket sales figures show that bananas are now the most popular fruit on the shelves. Although there are a thousand or so cultivated varieties of banana, it is the "Cavendish" variety which accounts for almost half of the 100 million tons of bananas grown world-wide. It is large, soft, sweet, yellow and easy to grow and harvest.

When my husband and I were in Africa we were introduced to a tasty variety which was small, firm, and slightly salty—and pink! Dan Koeppler, in his book about bananas, states that soon the consumer's appetite for new things will take over the banana trade and Cavendish fruit will have competition from other varieties.

When the Second World War had ended, and bananas reappeared in British shops, children had to be taught how to peel them! The one unmistakeable fact about a banana is that the goodness is on the inside. If you want to enjoy a banana, you have to open it up. An "unzipped" banana goes bad and does nobody any good.

We have a similar precious resource within our reach – it is the Bible! Just as the banana is of no use to those who refuse to open it, so the Bible cannot bring its life-changing truths to the human heart who fails to read it. You have to get inside the book to appreciate its goodness, to unzip the case and extract the pithy truth that is there in each and every chapter.

The Christian faith is no longer the most widely presented "fruit of the Spirit". However, it is vital that children are shown how to peel through stories and traditions and re discover the goodness of God inside the Bible—which is still one of the world's best sellers.

More than Money can Buy

I had a rich uncle, who started as an office boy in a textile mill and by dint of hard work—and an intriguing personality—rose through the ranks until one day he bought the mill! I knew he was rich because every time we met, he would give me half a crown. That was a coin of real stature in those days, two shillings and sixpence worth of status for a little girl!

I don't know what you think, but for me there seemed to be something safe and satisfying about our pre-decimal coinage. They felt solid; they had the security of the sovereign's face on the front and real character on the reverse of some coins. The farthing, for example, had a wren, whilst on the halfpenny there was a sailing ship in full rig, the three penny piece, gold coloured, had 12 sides. There was paper money, worth 10 shillings, £1 and £5, and oh the feel of those large white paper notes!

The value of money in those days was tangible. We knew back then that 240 pennies made one pound; but when the new decimalised coins came in, suddenly 100 pennies equalled one new pound—although the maths were simpler—the merchandise appeared to rise in value overnight!

I am writing this because I hear that very soon we are to have a new one pound coin, based on the shape of the old three penny bit—with 12 sides—and composed of two different coloured metals. But, I wonder by 2017 when the coin is introduced, what will we be able to buy with it? As prices rise, a pound might not be worth as much then as it is today.

I thank God for those things which money can never buy; things which never reduce in value. Our health and friendships; secure family and contentment; money might be able to help even in these things, but it cannot buy them—and the blessings they bring will continue long after money runs out, for these blessings are not maintained by material resources.

There are spiritual blessings too which come from God entirely free of charge. They are not out of the reach of the poorest, and they cannot be devalued by inflation! The Bible affirms:

> *"But godliness with contentment is great gain. For we brought nothing into the world, and we can take nothing out of it." (1 Timothy 6:6-7)*

Faith, hope and love do not carry a price tag—what we receive from God is priceless!

© Romrodinka | Dreamstime.com

Childhood Joy

My friend's son Timothy was eagerly anticipating his 4th birthday. Just a week to go and he was counting the days! Bouncing up and down, he explained how big he was going to be. "Big boys who are 4 years old can manage to sit still!" said his mother. Timothy is smart—as well as potentially big. "Mum," he explained, "today I'm still only 3. I'll sit still tomorrow when I'm 4!"

It seems that children grow up so quickly these days. When I am introduced to a small baby, already wearing denim, I am wistful for a previous generation of babies who wore baby clothes! When I meet a 5-year-old wielding a mobile phone with more skill than I have, I am wistful for little girls who carry dolls and little boys who wear pirate hats and order me to walk the plank.

I'm sure we want to give our children every advantage provided in this gadget-driven society, but we must take care not to deny them the opportunity to enjoy the excitement of their own imagination. Puddles are for splashing in, mud is for making mud pies, glue is for sticking paper and foxglove flowers are to wear on your fingers!

Children develop skills by exploring their environment. Motor skills precede the skills of reading and writing. Have you ever considered how much imagination is required to accept that black marks on a white page produce letters, words and convey meaning? The development of a child's body, mind and spirit need equal attention. Children can thrive in the atmosphere of worship. Psalm 100 announces: *"Make a joyful shout to the Lord, all you lands! Serve the Lord with gladness; Come before His presence with singing." (Psalm 100:1-2)*

I enjoy this delightful fable concerning Jesus:

> *When Jesus Christ was 4 years old, The angels brought him toys of gold, Which no man ever bought, or sold. And yet, with these He did not play. He made some small birds out of clay—Then blessed them, and they flew away.*

One day, when Timothy is fully grown, he will fly the nest of home and make his own way in the world. He will be blessed if he has learned to appreciate the wonders of the world. The greatest wonder of all is that the Maker of the universe is concerned for him and cares for him. And so he cares for you and I, too. A fully mature character is to be found in those who have learned to: "Be still, and know that I am God." (Psalm 46:10)

The Water of Life

The rain, once again, throws a veil round the valley,
The mountains in mist make our hills seem a plain;
The greyness and wetness of storm never ending,
Some spell it "Whales" on account of the rain.

Seventy-one per cent of our planet is water,
Just one per cent used for welfare of Man.
The greatest dilemma facing humanity
Is how to share water? It's vital we can.

Provide for all nations. In sun parched Botswana
The name for the currency is as the rain;
"Pula" the rain, and "Pula" the money -
Without the rain is no financial gain.

It's hard to imagine, from water logged valleys,
That earth can be blistered and arid, so dry;
That green growth is withered and animals perish
And there is no food, and the babies will die.

This all needs to change! Our planet is critical,
World water gaps widen, and hope falls right through.
The sound of the rain – hear it as tear drops
For three point four million people, who knew:

Thirst requires water; the water was dirty
But there was no other - so they bent to drink;
Killed by the water; no flush sanitation;
Most of the world makes the river its sink!

Intelligent governments, making decisions,
Changing its systems, need to rethink
How water is managed. In water rich Europe
There is no problem. We've plenty to drink.

But this is required in Southern Sahara,
Where the people make do with ten litres, no more.
Rain sodden Welshman, think of their dryness,
Hear Earths thirsty ones as they pound your hearts
door.

Change how we use water. Conserve it. Contain it.
Create from our plenty a further supply.
All water descends from the clouds, now we use it
Faster than nature renews to the sky.

For a change, let's be grateful when it is raining,
Let's change our response to this is heavenly gold.
Those valuable drops which quench mankind's
thirsting
Are a treasure which our Welsh skies certainly hold!

© Berniedheere| Dreamstime.com

Little is Much

There is a well-known story of a little Dutch boy who saved a multitude of people from drowning when he discovered a hole in the dyke wall which he plugged with his thumb until help arrived! He was in the right place at the right time. He also had the right attitude to the situation in which he found himself. "It's my responsibility to help if I can." Consider a different scenario. "There's a leak in the dyke. The wall will give way. The water will flood the valley. I must run for my life!" Do you think he would have been able to run fast enough and far enough to escape the deluge?

Consider the well-known story of David and Goliath. Two armies faced each other across a valley. The Philistine champion was a giant, three metres tall. He taunted the Israelite army. "Choose one man to come down here and fight me. If he kills me, then we will be your slaves. If I kill him, you will be our slaves. I defy the armies of Israel today!" When the King and the army heard this, they were terrified.

A boy named David was visiting his brothers who were soldiers in the army. He heard the giant's challenge and reacted in surprise. "Who is this pagan Philistine, anyway, who is allowed to defy the armies of the living God? I will go and fight him!" declared David. The king's response was "Don't be ridiculous!"

However, David persisted in his intention and he faced the giant. He killed him, with a shepherd boy's weapon of sling and stones. He had faith in the presence and power of Almighty God. He told the giant, "You come to me with sword, spear and javelin, but I come in the name of the Lord of Heaven's armies."

What do these two stories have in common? There was a desperate situation and both boys identified the need. They used what they had and they considered other people before themselves. They did not anticipate failure! They had faith.

We may feel small and insignificant, especially as we get older, but we are not! While God is with us we can never be redundant. No one is too small or insignificant for him to use. Enjoy these words from the Bible:

> "I have set the LORD continually before me; Because He is at my right hand, I will not be shaken. Therefore my heart is glad and my glory rejoices; My flesh also will dwell securely." (Psalm 16:8-9)

Half Empty or Half Full?

It seems that people can be divided into two categories: they are either optimists or pessimists. An optimist says, "The glass is half full!" whilst the pessimist declares, "The glass is half empty!" However, I am beginning to think that in society today there is no need to supply the glass, since most people think there is nothing to put in it, any way!

Every day our news programmes regale us with bleak facts and figures concerning unemployment, teenage violence, failing schools, Alzheimer's disease, distress in Residential homes, failure in the Health Service and the state of the economy. But what about those businesses which are flourishing, I ask; teenagers who are successful, schools with good results, wonderful advances in medical science, compassionate care for old people in many nursing homes, and the provision of free health care for everyone?

Some tell us that the government is effectively bankrupt, and that the financial situation can only get worse—yet all our pensions have been paid on time each month (so far at least)! The fact is that such good news exists, but sadly it hardly ever reaches the news headlines; and this is an unfortunate fact which seems to suggest that most people (in the media at least) are pessimists.

One might be forgiven for wondering if there is a conspiracy to hide the light of God's love and care for his creatures and enhance the darkness. When will this generation ever take time to count its blessings?

Someone reminded me recently of the story of a girl called Polly-Anna. As the story goes, her family were poor and any extra luxuries came in charity barrels. Polly-Anna yearned for a doll and when the next charity offering arrived, she was sure that there would be something special for her! But the only item for a child was a pair of small wooden crutches. She surveyed them, with tears in her eyes, before saying, in a wobbly voice, "Well, at least I can be glad I don't need them!"

When I consider these words from the Bible: "Do not be afraid or discouraged because of this vast army. For the battle is not yours, but God's...Go out to face them tomorrow, and the Lord will be with you" (from 2 Chronicles 20:15-17), I feel that the glass of a believer is full and running over!

© Paweł Szpytma | Dreamstime.com

The Impossible Axe

One day a group of workmen were busily cutting timber along the river bank when suddenly, an iron axe head flew of its handle and sank to the bottom of the river. The man who had been using the axe stopped and shouted, "It's not my axe! What shall we do?" The prophet, who was with the group, threw a piece of wood into the water; the axe head rose from the watery depths and was easily retrieved.

This is an amazing incident from the life of Elisha the prophet — but what on earth can we learn from an anecdote about a piece of iron which was made to float?

Firstly, notice that the workmen were accompanied by a prophet. I can remember a time in this country when chaplains were employed by most organisations and trades. A man of God was available when any crisis, great or small, occurred. The Bible is emphatic in its declaration that our God is a very present help in time of trouble.

I am convinced that people in our modern age are more—not less—in need of turning to God and his ministers in times of crisis. Yet it would be far better if they turned to him habitually and included him in their daily affairs. In the account of the floating axe head we read that one of the workers said, "Won't you please come with your servants?" God is always willing to partner us in our enterprise.

Secondly, notice that what happened to someone else's property mattered. If we have a concern for other people, then we reflect the heart of our compassionate God. Certainly, God is concerned about honesty in our lives, and so we should always return borrowed items. But more than that, the lesson must be that we are all affected by the blessings or misfortunes of others. We cannot get away from it, for we are 'our brother's keeper.'

And there is something else I am absolutely sure of: if we are prepared to act in faith according to God's word (as it was given in this instance by the prophet Elisha) we can still expect miracles when we place our affairs in the hands of God.

Iron that floats?! It may just be that your present situation seems even more impossible than that! Yet recall the words of the angel Gabriel:

> "For with God nothing will be impossible." (Luke 1:37 NKJV™)

Saving for a Donkey

Jacob was saving up his money to buy a donkey. He thought that if he only had a donkey then he would be able to travel much further and faster than he could on his own feet, and so he could earn a lot more money. Besides, he could rent the donkey out from time to time to other people who wanted to travel. He knew that a donkey would be expensive but it was a worthwhile project—a good investment—so he took any odd job that came his way in order to add his meagre wages to the donkey fund.

First, Jacob got a job washing a camel. This camel had been carrying leather bottles full of freshly pressed olive oil; but one of these bottles was leaking and olive oil had trickled out all over the camel's back. When a hot wind blew in from the desert, the sand stuck to the oil and coated the camel's back with a hard crust like sandpaper. The camel did not at all enjoy being washed and it showed its displeasure by stamping on Jacobs feet!

Next, Jacob got a job carrying oranges from the orange farm to the market. When one of the sacks split and the oranges went rolling down the hill into a clump of thorn bushes, Jacob was badly scratched by the sharp thorns.

At last Jacob found a job that he really liked. There was a pool in Jerusalem, with water deep enough for swimming and five arched porches with geraniums and roses growing over them. Many sick people sheltered under the porches, because from time to time the water would bubble and swirl and that was when an angel came and stirred the water with his wings. The first person to get in the water after that would be cured of his illness.

There were attendants waiting to help the sick and disabled— family members, mostly—and Jacob worked for a while as an assistant to a wealthy group of these attendants. Each day he swept around the pool, making sure that everything was fresh and tidy; he sometimes ran errands too, for the attendants were afraid to leave the pool in case the water was stirred in their absence.

After some time Jacob got to know some of the sick people quite well. There was one man who had been unable to walk for over 38 years. He had been coming to the pool all that time and yet he had never been able to get down into the water. He was brought by his relatives in the morning and they took him home each evening, but all day they left him alone on a mat under one of the porches. When Jacob saw how despondent and lonely the man was, he made a point of stopping each morning as he swept round the pool, just to spend a little time talking to the man.

Visitors to Jerusalem would often come to the pool of Bethesda, not only because it was such a beautiful pool, but also because they wanted to see whether miracle cures really did take place there; whether an angel really did come to help the people.

One day, Jesus of Nazareth walked down to the pool. Jacob had met Jesus before, when his family had been invited to a wedding in Cana in Galilee. At that wedding Jesus had turned gallons of water into fine tasting wine. Jacob never forgot a good wine, especially when it was free! So when Jacob recognised Jesus, he began to sweep very quickly round the pool, so that he was soon working near where Jesus was standing.

Jacob found Jesus stooping to talk to the man who had spent 38 years waiting beside the pool. "Do you want to get better?" Jesus asked the man. The man looked up at Jesus and replied, "What can I do about it? I have no attendant to help me get into the water when the angel stirs it with his wings."

Jesus answered him with a voice of command: "Get up! Pick up your mat and walk!"

The man looked at Jesus and then he looked at his poor, thin legs. He twisted the hem of his mat in his fingers, and then he looked up at Jesus again. Then, to Jacob's amazement, that man, who had been unable to walk for 38 years, stood up, rolled up his mat and walked away from the porch. He stood near the edge of the pool and laughed. "I'm cured!" he shouted as he skipped through the porch before the astonished crowds.

Jacob was very thoughtful as he continued his sweeping. "Just imagine that!" he thought to himself. "There were all these people here, but Jesus chose to cure this man who had no one else to help him. When I get enough money to buy my donkey, I want to ask Jesus to do me the honour of being the first man ever to ride on his back!"

And you'll never guess! That's exactly what did happen on the first Palm Sunday. Well, possibly...

The Fragrance of God

It seems that I have lost my sense of smell! The delightful, delicious, delectable fragrances of lavender, new mown grass, salty sea water, strawberries ripening in the summer sunshine, fresh baked bread, warm from the oven, frosty air, the comprehensive conglomerate perfume of Christmas, sizzling bacon, freshly ground coffee — all are redolent in my memory, but no longer realistic experiences! Of course, I also miss out on sour milk, sweaty feet, dirty drains and bad breath; but all the experiences of life are surely enriched by the collection of odours they contain.

Palm Sunday was a heady experience. Jerusalem was crowded for the Passover feast. The market tables full of oranges, lemons, dates, and figs vied in the aroma stakes with the powders and grains on the spice stalls. Entrepreneurs unrolled bales of cloth, exotic in a variety of colours and lovely to touch, each different material exuding a different scent. Camels, donkeys, children, Jews, Roman soldiers, visitors from other countries—at this time every year Jerusalem became a hodgepodge of sight, sound and smell.

Into this arena came Jesus, riding a donkey into the city of Jerusalem as the people waved palm branches and shouted:

"Hosanna to the Son of David! Blessed is he who comes in the name of the Lord! Hosanna in the highest heaven!" (Matt. 21:9)

If I had been there 2000 years ago, I would have cheered the Messiah on his way and I would have revelled in the sights and joined in the sound—but for me there would be no smell!

With this in mind, let us consider the following verse from the Bible:

"But thanks be to God, who always leads us as captives in Christ's triumphal procession and uses us to spread the aroma of the knowledge of him everywhere. For we are to God the pleasing aroma of Christ among those who are being saved and those who are perishing." (2 Corinthians 2:14-15)

However secure we might be in our present situation, if we do not recognise the fragrance of faith — then our living is less than complete. And our own incompleteness will affect the society in which we live.

Sweeping the Roads for God

The postman always used to arrive at our house before breakfast with another delivery after lunch. The mail was a regular and dependable feature of everyday life and the postman became a neighbourhood friend. But now e-mails and mobile texts are taking over. The red phone box has been superseded by a mobile phone which fits in the palm of your hand.

We have a friend who is a photographer and his years of training, excellent qualifications and delightful artistic skills are challenged by digital cameras—even a mobile phone can produce clear and acceptable pictures these days.

The ambitious mechanism of a modern washing machine has already rendered obsolete the musical weekly list of domestic chores; no longer is Monday wash day, we can look neat and charming every day! There was nothing neat or charming about posser sticks (do you remember those?), flat irons on the fire and dripping washing in the kitchen because it was raining again!

There is one job which hasn't changed although possibly the job description has. We still have road sweepers! They sweep away rubbish and make our environment safe and attractive. They were once called "Length Men". Each "Length Man" was responsible for a certain number of roads; he had his own allocated area to keep clean.

Now, here is a challenge for you! Can you become a "Length Man" for God? Would you be willing to carry the sweeping brush of prayer and with it, make it your daily responsibility to sweep clean your immediate neighbourhood by presenting people, places, problems, pains - and potentials for good -- to God in prayer? There is only one essential requirement if you want to have this noble job—you must believe in the presence of God and in prayer. Then you take the brush called faith and use it with success and satisfaction.

The Bible explains it like this:

> "The Lord bless you and keep you; the Lord make his
> face shine on you and be gracious to you; the Lord
> turn his face toward you and give you peace."
> (Numbers 6:24-25)

Times are changing; but maybe the change most needed is a return to the time when prayer was a regular feature of daily living.

© Wam1975 | Dreamstime.com

The Changing Seasons

September is a beautiful month. The various shades of summer green change into the rich hues of amber, bronze, ochre and mustard yellow. Red leaves vie with the brilliance of dahlias and chrysanthemums to colour the gardens with autumn fire. Apples, blackberries, late raspberries and plentiful beans fill the allotments. Rosy sunsets promise more sun filled days. The declaration made thousands of years ago continues to be true. "As long as the earth remains there will be seedtime and harvest, cold and heat, summer and winter, day and night."

What comes next? Already the plenitude of autumn is being hidden by a forecast of winter's hardness. The cold of winter reflects the chill of fear in some hearts today. "Heating or food?" is a cry which has already provoked Food Bank providers in the UK to express concern about their ability to meet the needs of low income families. Dark winter mornings provoke fear among parents for the safety of their children walking to school at a time when school crossing patrols have been reduced. There seems to be nothing but the chill of winter in human nature when we focus only on problems or hazards. We must do so, of course, but not to the extent that we forget hope or happiness!

When you stop to think, we have many blessings which other countries lack. We have freedom to worship God according to our conscience. Our children receive free education in good schools with a wide and varied curriculum and opportunities to develop every skill. As older people we receive free health care, pensions and when needed, residential homes which offer compassion and kindness. We have a lot to be thankful for after all!

More than that, we are living at a time when scientists are making amazing discoveries concerning the very fabric of creation. One of the Psalms poses this question: "When I consider the heavens, the moon and the stars which you have ordained—what is man?" Surely the answer is given in the introduction to the Lord's Prayer—"Our Father in Heaven". What a blessing, to realise that we can be among the children of God!

It is a beautiful fact that God's calculations for the entire history of the world include His love and care for you and me. The winter of our discontent comes when we forget this amazing blessing of divine love.

© Brian Arbuthnot| Dreamstime.com

Singing in the Dark

Someone has just sent to me a charming article from a London evening paper, which describes robins singing in the dark. Perplexed by a continual bird song through a bleak winter's night, the writer of the article had appealed to the Royal Society for the Protection of Birds for some information, and this is what she was told:

> *"Seeming to think that artificial lighting means the sun is rising, robins, who are the most territorial of birds, and who will fight to the death to protect their boundaries, have decided they had better get on and mark out territory even at two in the morning. They are motivated by their plainness. Being less showy than other woodland birds they have to make more effort with their voices. They also have the best songs!"*

Christians are people who have such a song in their hearts that the music of faith rings out in the darkest situations. They are intensely anxious to protect the boundaries of their belief in Jesus Christ, the Son of God, who came to be the Saviour of the world. Knowing that their strength comes from Christ, and that they have no glory of their own—they sing for him! The plain truth is that the Christ, who is in me and who alone is my glory, is the reason why I sing!

Christians have the best songs!

I do not mean lyrically or in terms of musical composition. I refer instead to the way in which they express the hope, joy, peace, forgiveness and other qualities of life which are the inheritance of those who put their trust in God. The blessings which God gives us do not change like our outward circumstances; so we are able to sing and rejoice in even the toughest events of life. We sometimes call this experience "having a song in the night."

Here is some good advice from Psalm 42:

By day the Lord directs his love, at night his song is with me—a prayer to the God of my life. Why, my soul, are you downcast? Why so disturbed within me? Put your hope in God, for I will yet praise him, my Savior and my God. (Psalm 42:8,11)

Sing a song for Jesus, and bring the melody of God's love into whatever discordant situation you may face today!

The Found Sheep

There is a well-known story about a shepherd who had a hundred sheep and who lost one of them! So he left the ninety-nine sheep and went looking for the one sheep that was lost.

Whenever I hear this story I have many questions. Did the shepherd lose the sheep or did the sheep lose itself? What was so special about this one sheep that the shepherd should be concerned to find it again? Is there economic sense in valuing one creature above ninety-nine others?

It would appear that the sheep lost itself, but if so--how and why? Was it self-willed, ignoring the boundaries of the field and the discipline of the flock? Did it run away to escape from danger? Was it afraid and looking for a safe place to hide? Did it get stuck in a bramble patch or in a ditch, unable to get out? Was it sick or weary?

Given that in the story the flock of sheep represent the herd of humanity, all these are rational reasons why the sheep might have got lost.

So what was special about this one sheep? Why, surely, nothing but the fact that it was lost, and separated from the flock and the shepherd. For whatever reason, and for whatever circumstances, this sheep was isolated, in need of support, hopeless and helpless.

Concerning the economics of the situation, wisdom might have decided that the safety of the ninety-nine sheep in the fold was more important than the well-being of one sheep that got lost! Yet the decisive factor in the story is the personality of the shepherd. He was a good shepherd who cared for *every* sheep in the flock.

I guess that lost sheep made urgent bleating when it recognised its lost state! Wherever you are today, if you recognise your lost state and call out to God for forgiveness in Jesus name, he will hear and forgive you.

God is listening for you and He is concerned for your well-being. God really, truly cares for you; he has infinite patience with all his creatures. Enjoy again the closing verse of Psalm 23, the Shepherd's psalm.

> *"Surely your goodness and love will follow me all the days of my life, and I will dwell in the house of the Lord forever."*

Don't Worry!

One day a little boy announced to his mother that in the school concert, he was going to play the part of a book. "I need a book costume!" he told his perplexed Mum. So his mum decided to go up to the school and discuss this with his teacher; after all, there are many kinds of books and such an outfit did not easily spring to mind.

When the mother explained her dilemma, she was greeted with a broad smile and the explanation, "He isn't a book — he is a page-boy!"

How often have I made the same mistake? When an unexpected event occurs, I immediately transfer the circumstances out of that one day, into a week, a month, or even a lifetime ahead! Instead of the page which is called today, I anticipate the whole book entitled, "What If?" In this way I can condemn myself to accept the uniform of worry and fearfulness instead of trust and praise.

The Bible advises us:

"Therefore do not worry about tomorrow, for tomorrow will worry about itself. Each day has enough trouble of its own." *(Matthew 6:34)*

The trouble is that we tend to write the entire story when we are, as it were, just on page one. When we become more concerned with the things that we are worried might happen, even though they are not actually happening, rather than with what is happening, we forget the part of the Bible called Lamentations which declares:

> *"Because of the Lord's great love we are not consumed, for his compassions never fail. They are new every morning; great is your faithfulness."* *(Lamentations 3:22-23)*

Beside our house there is an old oak tree which shelters a family of wrens. Each icy cold morning with snow blanketing the paths—a wren has been singing. After all, it is quite safe. The oak tree provides shelter and there is a new day to explore!

Faith sings whatever the weather and however chilly the situation. Faith can say,

> *"I say to myself, "The Lord is my portion; therefore I will wait for him." (Lamentations 3:24)*

In The Deep Midwinter

Snow has indeed fallen, snow on snow; so deep and crisp and even that people with recent Christmas carols in their memories might have been looking out for Good King Wenceslas! The blue moon is shining brightly, bringing a silvery light which enhances the beauty of the winter landscape. The cold has been cruel, though, and according to the weather forecasters, the low temperatures are likely to continue.

Depressing news was circulating concerning a lack of gas supplies, and every supermarket was full of shoppers—filling their trolleys as if we were living in Siberia instead of Wales—clearly imagining that there might be a shortage of supplies as more roads became impassable and traffic slowed to a standstill. But if winter comes—can spring be far behind?

I once heard an anecdote about a small girl who hurried home from school and said to her Mum, "I'm a cornflake in the

Christmas concert and you've got to dress me in bright yellow!" Mum was doubtful, but the child insisted that she was to be a bright yellow cornflake, so Mum and Grandma got to work and produced an outfit that was gloriously bright and beautiful. Came the afternoon of the performance, however, and when the children skipped onto the stage—everyone else was a white snowflake and there was just one radiant yellow cornflake!

I am grateful for the mistake! One cornflake made a great impact on that occasion, and one person, radiant amongst a concentration of cold situations and circumstances will also make a noticeable difference.

There is a modern hymn with this chorus: "Shine, Jesus, shine, fill this land with the Father's glory." God's light shining in our hearts can cause others to receive the light of his glory.

Not so long ago there was a well-used slogan going around some churches which suggested, "Smile, Jesus loves you!" If God's light shining in our hearts means we have a sunny personality then we can truly make a difference to all whom we come into contact with.

The Bible declares, "If God is for us, who can be against us?" (Rom. 8:31) and that's why one person (with God!) can really make a difference. Might that one person be you?

Great Orme in Sunshine

The Great Orme in the sunshine,
A lovely summer's day;
With fold on fold of mountains
Clear across the light filled bay.

Down the Orme slopes, names and slogans
Marked in stones of grey and white,
Commemorating visits, make
Graffiti kind and right.

Twanging up its cable,
As Llandudno drops below,
The tram pulls in. Nostalgic ride –
All transport once was slow.

Shopping precinct, rush and bustle;
Why acquiesce to hectic pace?
Is it worth our frantic efforts
To keep up with the human race?

As we turn into the main street,
Pavement cafe, custom slow;
Rain is threatening, maybe most folk
Think it best to buy and go.

But underneath a dripping cover,
One small boy begins to sing.
Childish voice, in Welsh, his solo
Might turn winter into spring.

More from Faithbuilders Publishing:

Faithbuilders Bible Study: The Gospel of Matthew

Faithbuilders Bible Study: The Gospel of Mark

The Pentecostal Bible Commentary Series: 1 Corinthians

The Prophet of Messiah

The Blessings of God's Grace

The Message of Mark

The Prophecy of Amos – A Warning for Today

More from Doreen Harrison

The Donkey Boy

Jubilant Jeremy Johnson

A Book of Bible Stories